PUBLIC LIBRARY OF JOHNSTON COUNTY
AND SMITHFIELD-SMITHFIELD, NC

W9-BLQ-071

Who wrote this story?

The Greeks told it long ago.

. . . arktos!

. . . ursa!

The Romans told it, too.

I've told it in a starlit way,
    Just
        for
            you.

Jean Marzollo

. . . bear!

for Patrick Finbarr Bowe

Dear Parents and Teachers,

The Greek myth of Callisto and Arcas is longer and more complicated
than the one I have simplified here for young children. As they grow
older, please encourage kids to read other, more detailed versions. Since
this story is thousands of years old, they will find it told in different,
fascinating ways by various storytellers.

Jean Marzollo

Grateful thanks to the Roman writer Ovid and to the ancient Greeks for
their inspiration, and to all the children, artists, and teachers who helped
me with this book, especially Dr. Joanne Marien, superintendent of
Somers School District in Somers, New York, and Bill Mayer, professor
of Classical Studies at Hunter College, New York City.

Copyright © 2005 by Jean Marzollo

All rights reserved.

Little, Brown and Company • Time Warner Book Group
1271 Avenue of the Americas, New York, NY 10020
Visit our Web site at www.lb-kids.com

First Edition: September 2005

Library of Congress Cataloging-in-Publication Data

Marzollo, Jean.
Little Bear, you're a star! : a Greek myth / retold and illustrated by Jean Marzollo.— 1st ed.
    p. cm.
  ISBN 0-316-74135-3
  1. Zeus (Greek deity)—Juvenile literature. 2. Mythology, Greek—Juvenile literature.
3. Ursa Major—Juvenile literature. 4. Ursa Minor-Juvenile literature. 5. Constellations—
Juvenile literature. I. Title.
  BL820.J8M27 2005
  398.2'0938'06—dc22   2004021271

10 9 8 7 6 5 4 3 2 1

SC

Printed in China

The illustrations for this book were painted in watercolor and Chinese ink, then scanned
and finished in Adobe Photoshop on a Power Mac G4. The text was set in
Hadriano Bold and Kid Print, and the display type was set in Galahad.

The ancient Greeks drew pictures on vases.   What does "ancient" mean?   Long, long ago.   Are we in this story?

A GREEK MYTH

Retold and Illustrated by JEAN MARZOLLO

Little Bear, You're a Star!

C LIBRARY OF JOHNSTON COUNTY
SMITHFIELD-SMITHFIELD, NC

LITTLE, BROWN AND COMPANY
New York ⁓ Boston

Yes, we're the Greek chorus! What's that? We listen to what's going on and then we talk about it. *Tweet!*

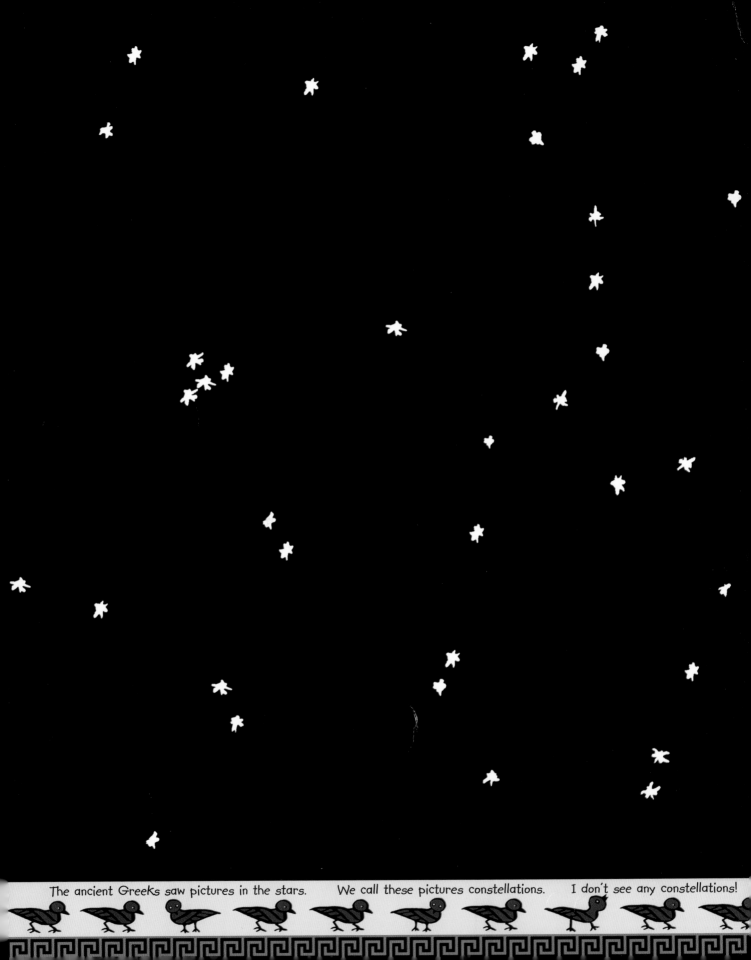

The ancient Greeks saw pictures in the stars.   We call these pictures constellations.   I don't see any constellations!

Come back and look after the story.   Will I see constellations then?   *Tweet!*

Way, way, way up high in the clouds, on a mountain called Mount Olympus, lived the Greek gods. The king of the gods was Zeus. The queen of the gods was Hera.

King Zeus noticed that way, way, way down on Earth there was a beautiful woman named Callisto. Zeus flew down to visit her. Callisto had a baby named Arcas.

Queen Hera decided to change
Callisto into an animal so
King Zeus wouldn't
visit her anymore.

I'm going to change you into a . . . into a . . .

Into a what?　　　　She's thinking, she's thinking.　　　*Tweet!*

. . . into a bear!

Callisto was a very nice bear, but her son, Arcas,
didn't understand that.

WAA!
WAA-AA!

If my mother turned into a bear, I would cry, too!   Tweet!

Kind people found Arcas and took him home with them.
Callisto was glad that they were so nice.

Roar!

Night fell. Callisto didn't know what bears
ate or where they slept. She did know
one thing, though. She knew she would
always love her son, Arcas, and that
she would stay nearby and
watch as he grew up.

Callisto misses her bed.   And she misses the warm fire in her cottage.   Most of all, she misses Arcas!   *Tweet!*

As time passed, Callisto began to enjoy being a bear. She learned to pick blueberries with her lips and tongue. Delicious! She also learned to eat grass and ants, though they weren't quite so tasty. As the months went by, Callisto watched her son, Arcas, learn to walk. She was very proud of him.

Personally, I think beaks are better than lips for picking blueberries.   But bears eat tons of blueberries!   *Tweet!*

Callisto learned to growl and roar. She roared to keep bees from stinging her nose whenever she helped herself to honey from their hives. But she never roared when her son, Arcas, was near, because she didn't want to frighten him. Sometimes she sat very quietly in the trees so she could listen to him sing.

You can sing this to the tune of "Twinkle, Twinkle, Little Star."

Birdie, Birdie in the sky,
How I wonder how you fly!

I don't like honey.   Me, neither. It makes my *beak* stick together.   Can bears really climb trees?   Yes!   *Tweet!*

Arcas learned to catch fish. Callisto learned
to catch fish, too.

Do you think that Arcas knows there's a bear nearby?   No.   Do you think Callisto knows where her son is?   *Tweet!*

Then, Arcas learned to hunt. Callisto watched with fear. She didn't like to see her son hunt her animal friends.

Run away, rabbit, run away!   Run away, squirrels, too!   *Tweet!*

Some mornings Callisto growled a hushed warning when Arcas came to hunt. The animals heard—and ran away.

Where are all the animals today? I don't see any of them!

One day King Zeus looked down on Earth to see how Arcas and Callisto were doing. He saw that, without knowing it, Arcas was about to shoot his mother!

This will be my first bear!

. . . into a bear!

Arcas was surprised to find himself getting a bear hug from a bear. Then, he realized that he was a bear, too!

Big Bear growled with happiness. Little Bear understood and growled back! Big Bear told Little Bear how she had once been his human mother. Little Bear told Big Bear that he had always sensed that there was someone watching over him as he grew up.

Growl!

Roar!

Roar!

Growl! Roar!
Roar!

What about the nice people who took care of Arcas? Zeus sent them another baby so they wouldn't miss Arcas so much. *Tweet!*

King Zeus decided that Big Bear and Little Bear should stay safely together forever. So, with a flash of lightning, he turned the bears into stars and tossed them by their tails into the sky. The last star Zeus touched was at the end of Little Bear's tail.

This star will be famous, Little Bear. It will be the only star that never moves as the seasons change. I will put it in the north sky, and people will call it the North Star. They will use it to find their way when they are lost. As they find their way, they will remember how you and Big Bear found each other.

Their tails look longer now.   Yes, they stretched a bit when Zeus put the bears in the sky.   Did that hurt?   No.

Roar!

Roar!

Do the bears miss being real bears? No, they love being star bears, together forever and ever. Shining down on Earth! *Tweet!*

Star Gazer's Guide;
After you look at this picture,
go back to the star picture
in the front of the book.
Can you find Big Bear and Little
Bear? Keep in mind that the
handles of the Dippers are
the tails of the bears!

Big Bear
(also called
Ursa Major)

Big Dipper
(7 stars)

Little Bear
(also called
Ursa Minor)

Little
Dipper
(7 stars)

North Star
(also call Polestar and Polaris)
If you can find the North Star,
you will always Know where north is.

5

4

3

2

Hint: To find the North Star,
go five times the distance between the
front two stars of the Big Dipper.

The North Star!   Yes, and Zeus gave that to . . . ?   Little Bear!   Tweet!

Parent/Teacher Guide

This story is written for young children.
Young children can learn that "north"
is a place on the globe where polar
bears live and where the North Pole is.

The abstract concept of north as a direction,
however, is not usually understood by children
before the ages of 7 to 8. Thus, children's understanding
of this story deepens as they grow.

Geography Question:
Which state flag has Big Bear and the
North Star on it?

(Alaska)

Word Lover's Guide:
"Arktos," the Greek word for "bear," gives us the
words "Arctic" (land around the North Pole)
and "arctophile" (a teddy bear collector).

Dramatic Enrichment:
The people of ancient Greece put on wonderful plays.
After children become familiar with this
story, they can take parts and read it like a play.
Non-readers can *roar* and *tweet* on cue.

I wonder who will take my part in the play?   Someone who likes to ask questions!   *Tweet!*

JOHNSTON CO. PUBLIC LIBRARY SYSTEM

3 8950 60924 5123

PUBLIC LIBRARY OF JOHNSTON COUNTY
AND SMITHFIELD-SMITHFIELD, NC

E Marzollo
Marzollo, Jean.
Little Bear, you're a star! : a
  Greek myth about the

WITHDRAWN

**Public Library of
Johnston County and Smithfield
Smithfield, NC**